From Instinct to Influence: Unraveling Human Behavior

Jamie Olsen

Copyright © [2023]

Author: Jamie Olsen

Title: From Instinct to Influence: Unraveling Human Behavior

All rights reserved. No part of this book may be reproduced or transmitted in any form or by any means, electronic or mechanical, including photocopying, recording, or by any information storage and retrieval system, without permission in writing from the author.

This book is a product of [Publisher's Jamie Olsen]

ISBN:

TABLE OF CONTENTS

Chapter 1: Introduction　　　　　　　　06

Understanding Human Behavior

The Significance of Studying Human Behavior

Chapter 2: The Basics of Human Behavior　10

Nature vs. Nurture: The Influence on Behavior

The Role of Genetics in Shaping Human Behavior

Environmental Factors and Their Impact on Behavior

Chapter 3: The Biological Foundations of Behavior　　　　　　　　　　　　　　　　17

The Brain: The Control Center of Behavior

Neurotransmitters and Their Effects on Behavior

Hormones and Behavior: The Endocrine System's Influence

Chapter 4: The Psychological Factors in Human Behavior　　　　　　　　　　　　　23

Personality Traits and Their Impact on Behavior

Cognitive Processes and Decision Making

Emotional Intelligence and Its Role in Behavior

Chapter 5: Social Influences on Human Behavior   30

Socialization and Its Effects on Behavior

Conformity and Obedience: The Power of Peer Pressure

The Impact of Culture on Behavior

Chapter 6: Developmental Psychology and Behavior   37

Childhood Development and Its Influence on Behavior

Adolescence and the Challenges of Behavioral Changes

Aging and Its Effects on Behavior

Chapter 7: Abnormal Behavior: Causes and Treatments   44

Understanding Psychological Disorders

The Biological and Environmental Factors in Mental Illness

Therapeutic Approaches to Treating Abnormal Behavior

Chapter 8: The Role of Motivation in Human Behavior   50

Intrinsic and Extrinsic Motivation

Maslow's Hierarchy of Needs and Behavior

Goal Setting and Achievement: The Power of Motivation

Chapter 9: The Influence of Media on Human Behavior 56

Media Consumption and Its Effects on Behavior

Advertising and Consumer Behavior

The Impact of Social Media on Behavior

Chapter 10: The Future of Human Behavior Studies 62

Advancements in Neuroscience and Behavior Research

Ethical Considerations in Studying Human Behavior

Applying Behavioral Insights for Personal and Societal Growth

Chapter 11: Conclusion 68

Recap of Key Findings

Implications for Understanding and Influencing Human Behavior

Chapter 1: Introduction

Understanding Human Behavior

Human behavior is a complex and fascinating subject that encompasses a wide range of factors and influences. In order to navigate the intricacies of human behavior, it is essential to delve into the various aspects that shape our actions, thoughts, and emotions. This subchapter aims to provide a comprehensive understanding of human behavior, shedding light on its underlying mechanisms and exploring the factors that contribute to its formation.

At its core, human behavior is driven by a combination of innate instincts and external influences. These instincts are deeply rooted in our evolutionary past and have been shaped by millions of years of adaptation. They serve as the foundation for our basic needs, such as survival, reproduction, and social interactions. Understanding these primal instincts is crucial for comprehending why we behave in certain ways, even in modern society.

However, human behavior is not solely determined by instincts. Our actions are also heavily influenced by various external factors, including culture, upbringing, education, and socialization. These factors provide the framework within which our instincts are expressed, shaping our beliefs, values, and attitudes. By studying the interplay between nature and nurture, we gain valuable insights into the complex nature of human behavior.

Furthermore, human behavior is influenced by cognitive processes, such as perception, memory, and decision-making. These processes play a vital role in how we interpret and respond to the world around us. By examining the cognitive mechanisms that underlie our behavior, we gain a deeper understanding of why we think and act the way we do.

In addition to instincts, external influences, and cognitive processes, emotions also play a significant role in human behavior. Our emotional experiences shape our responses and guide our decision-making, often overriding rational thought. Understanding the emotional aspect of behavior allows us to comprehend the motivations and reactions that drive our actions.

Ultimately, understanding human behavior is a multidimensional endeavor that requires the integration of various fields, including psychology, sociology, biology, and neuroscience. By exploring the intricate connections between nature, nurture, cognition, and emotions, we can unravel the complexities of human behavior and gain valuable insights into ourselves and others.

Whether you are a student of psychology, a professional in the field, or simply someone intrigued by human behavior, this subchapter will provide a comprehensive overview of the factors that shape our actions, thoughts, and emotions. By delving into the depths of understanding human behavior, we can unlock the keys to self-awareness, empathy, and influence, enabling us to navigate the complexities of the human experience.

The Significance of Studying Human Behavior

Human behavior is a fascinating subject that holds immense significance in our lives. Understanding why we behave the way we do and deciphering the intricacies of human behavior can provide valuable insights into various aspects of our lives. From personal relationships to professional success, studying human behavior can have a profound impact on our overall well-being.

One of the key reasons why studying human behavior is crucial is that it helps us comprehend our own actions and reactions. By gaining insight into our motivations, thoughts, and emotions, we can make conscious decisions that align with our values and goals. This self-awareness allows us to navigate through life's challenges more effectively and develop a deeper understanding of ourselves.

Moreover, studying human behavior also enhances our ability to empathize with others. As social beings, our interactions with others play a vital role in shaping our experiences. By understanding the behavior of those around us, we can foster stronger relationships, build trust, and create a positive impact on the people we encounter. Empathy enables us to connect on a deeper level, leading to more meaningful and fulfilling connections.

In addition, studying human behavior is essential in the professional realm. Whether you are a leader, manager, or team member, understanding how individuals think and behave can greatly influence your success in the workplace. By recognizing patterns, motivations, and communication styles, you can adapt your approach to work harmoniously with others and create a conducive environment for collaboration and productivity.

Furthermore, studying human behavior can contribute to personal growth and development. It enables us to identify and overcome destructive patterns, such as unhealthy habits or negative thought processes. By studying behavior, we can learn strategies to manage stress, improve communication, and cultivate positive habits that support our mental, emotional, and physical well-being.

Lastly, studying human behavior has significance on a societal level. By understanding the factors that drive human behavior, we can address social issues more effectively. It can help us develop policies, interventions, and programs that promote positive change and improve the overall quality of life for individuals and communities.

In conclusion, studying human behavior is significant for everyone. It empowers us with self-awareness, enhances our interpersonal relationships, improves our professional success, fosters personal growth, and contributes to positive societal change. By unraveling the complexities of human behavior, we can create a more compassionate, understanding, and harmonious world.

Chapter 2: The Basics of Human Behavior

Nature vs. Nurture: The Influence on Behavior

Introduction:

Human behavior has always been a fascinating subject of study, prompting numerous debates and discussions. One of the most intriguing questions in this field revolves around the influence of nature and nurture on our behavior. Are we born with certain predispositions, or is our behavior shaped entirely by our environment? In this subchapter, we delve into the compelling nature vs. nurture debate, exploring how both factors play a significant role in shaping human behavior.

The Role of Nature:

Nature refers to our genetic makeup and the inherent traits we are born with. Our genes provide a blueprint for various physical and psychological characteristics. From eye color to intelligence, nature plays a significant role in determining who we are. Certain behaviors and tendencies, such as introversion or extroversion, may also be influenced by our genetic predispositions. These inherent traits act as a foundation upon which our behavior develops.

The Influence of Nurture:

Nurture, on the other hand, pertains to the impact of our environment, including our upbringing, education, and social interactions. Our experiences mold our behavior and shape our personalities. From childhood to adulthood, we learn from our surroundings, imitating others and adapting to societal norms. Our behavior can be heavily influenced by our family dynamics, cultural background, peer groups, and even the media we consume. Nurture acts as a powerful force that can either reinforce or challenge our genetic predispositions.

The Interplay between Nature and Nurture:

It is crucial to understand that nature and nurture are not mutually exclusive but instead interact in a complex manner. Our genetic makeup can influence how we respond to our environment, while our environment can, in turn, modify our genetic expression. For example, a person may have a genetic predisposition for aggression, but if they grow up in a nurturing and supportive environment, they may develop more prosocial behaviors.

The Implications for Understanding Human Behavior:

Recognizing the interplay between nature and nurture is vital for understanding human behavior comprehensively. It allows us to appreciate the complexity of our actions, acknowledging that both genetic and environmental factors contribute to who we are. By studying this interplay, we gain insights into how behavior is shaped and can identify strategies to nurture positive behaviors or intervene in negative ones.

Conclusion:

In this subchapter, we have explored the nature vs. nurture debate and its influence on human behavior. While nature provides us with inherent traits, nurture molds and refines these traits through our experiences and environment. Understanding the interplay between nature and nurture allows us to have a more holistic view of human behavior, recognizing the multidimensional factors that contribute to our actions. By unraveling this intricate relationship, we can better understand ourselves and others, leading to a more compassionate and empathetic approach towards behavior.

The Role of Genetics in Shaping Human Behavior

Genetics plays a significant role in shaping human behavior, influencing various aspects of our lives, from personality traits to predispositions for certain behaviors. In this subchapter, we will explore the fascinating connection between genetics and human behavior, shedding light on how our DNA can impact our actions and decisions.

One of the fundamental aspects of human behavior influenced by genetics is personality traits. Numerous studies have shown that certain traits, such as extroversion or introversion, are heritable to some extent. This means that our genetic makeup can predispose us to be more outgoing or reserved in social settings. Furthermore, genetics can also influence other personality dimensions, such as openness to new experiences, conscientiousness, and emotional stability.

In addition to personality traits, genetics also plays a role in shaping our behavior through the inheritance of specific genes that are associated with certain behaviors. For instance, genes related to aggression have been identified and linked to a higher likelihood of engaging in aggressive behavior. Similarly, genes associated with addiction can increase an individual's susceptibility to substance abuse.

Moreover, genetics can also influence our behavior by affecting our cognitive abilities and intellectual capacity. Studies have shown that genes are involved in intelligence and can contribute to variations in cognitive functions, such as memory, attention, and problem-solving skills. While environmental factors also play a crucial role in cognitive development, genetics provide the foundation upon which these abilities are built.

It is important to note that genetics does not solely determine our behavior. Nature and nurture interact in complex ways, and the interplay between our genetic makeup and environmental factors is crucial. Various studies have highlighted the significance of gene-environment interactions, demonstrating that genetic predispositions can be influenced and modified by the environment we grow up in.

Understanding the role of genetics in shaping human behavior can have profound implications for society. It can help debunk myths surrounding behavior, emphasizing that it is not solely a matter of personal choice or willpower. Recognizing the genetic factors at play can lead to more empathy and understanding, promoting a more compassionate approach to behaviors that might otherwise be stigmatized.

In conclusion, genetics undoubtedly plays a significant role in shaping human behavior. Our genetic makeup influences our personality traits, predispositions to certain behaviors, cognitive abilities, and more. However, it is essential to remember that genetics is not the sole determinant of behavior, and the interplay between nature and nurture is crucial. By understanding the role of genetics in behavior, we can gain a deeper appreciation for the complexity of human nature and foster a more inclusive and empathetic society.

Environmental Factors and Their Impact on Behavior

Introduction:
The intricate relationship between the environment and human behavior is a fascinating subject that has intrigued scholars and researchers for centuries. In this subchapter, we delve into the various environmental factors that play a crucial role in shaping human behavior. By understanding these factors, we gain valuable insights into the complexities of human nature and how external forces influence our actions. Whether you are a curious individual seeking to unravel the mysteries of human behavior or a professional in the field of behavior analysis, this subchapter will provide you with a comprehensive overview of the impact of environmental factors on behavior.

The Power of the Environment:
The environment in which we live and interact exerts a profound influence on our thoughts, emotions, and actions. From the physical surroundings to societal norms and cultural values, every aspect of our environment shapes our behavior in unique ways. For instance, research has shown that individuals who grow up in impoverished neighborhoods are more likely to engage in criminal activities due to limited access to resources and opportunities. Similarly, the presence of green spaces and nature has been linked to improved mental well-being and reduced stress levels.

Social Influences:
Humans are inherently social beings, and our behavior is greatly influenced by the people around us. The subchapter explores the impact of social factors such as peer pressure, family dynamics, and

societal expectations on our actions. For instance, teenagers often adopt the behaviors and attitudes of their peer group to fit in, leading to conformity and sometimes unhealthy behaviors. Understanding these social influences is crucial for parents, educators, and policymakers in creating environments that foster positive behavior and discourage negative influences.

Cultural and Historical Factors:
Culture and history shape our perceptions, values, and beliefs, which in turn influence our behavior. This section explores how cultural norms, traditions, and historical events shape our actions and interactions. Differences in behavior between cultures can be attributed to variations in environmental factors, such as the importance placed on individualism versus collectivism. By recognizing and appreciating these cultural and historical influences, we can develop a better understanding of human behavior across diverse populations.

Conclusion:
Environmental factors are powerful determinants of human behavior. By recognizing and understanding the impact of the environment on behavior, we can gain valuable insights into ourselves and others. Whether you are an individual seeking personal growth or a professional in the field of behavior analysis, this subchapter provides a comprehensive exploration of the influence of environmental factors on behavior. Armed with this knowledge, we can begin to unravel the intricate complexities of human behavior and work towards creating environments that foster positive change.

Chapter 3: The Biological Foundations of Behavior

The Brain: The Control Center of Behavior

The human brain is an extraordinary organ that serves as the control center for all our behaviors. From the moment we wake up in the morning to the time we go to sleep at night, our brain is constantly working behind the scenes, orchestrating our thoughts, emotions, and actions. In this subchapter, we will delve into the fascinating realm of the brain and explore how it shapes our behavior.

At its core, the brain is composed of billions of specialized cells called neurons. These neurons communicate with each other through electrical impulses and chemical signals, forming intricate networks that allow us to think, feel, and interact with the world around us. It is within these networks that the magic of behavior unfolds.

One of the fundamental aspects of behavior that the brain controls is our instincts. Instincts are innate patterns of behavior that are essential for our survival and are hardwired into our brains. From our instinct to seek food and water to our instinct to protect ourselves when faced with danger, these automatic responses are deeply rooted in the primitive parts of our brain.

However, our behavior is not solely determined by instincts. The brain is also highly adaptable and has the remarkable ability to learn and change throughout our lives. This phenomenon is known as neuroplasticity. Through a process of rewiring and reorganizing its neural connections, the brain can acquire new knowledge, develop new skills, and modify existing behaviors.

Moreover, our brain is heavily influenced by external factors such as our environment and experiences. These external influences shape our behavior and can have a profound impact on our thoughts, emotions, and actions. From early childhood experiences to cultural norms and societal expectations, our brain is constantly being shaped by the world around us.

Understanding the intricate workings of the brain is crucial for unraveling human behavior. By studying the brain, scientists and researchers can gain insights into various behavioral disorders, such as anxiety, depression, and addiction, and develop effective treatments and interventions.

In conclusion, the brain is the control center of our behavior, orchestrating our every thought, emotion, and action. From instinctual behaviors that ensure our survival to the adaptive changes that occur through learning and experience, the brain plays a pivotal role in shaping who we are. By unraveling the mysteries of the brain, we can gain a deeper understanding of human behavior and pave the way for a better future.

Neurotransmitters and Their Effects on Behavior

Understanding human behavior is a complex task that requires exploring the intricate workings of our brains. One crucial aspect of this exploration involves studying neurotransmitters and their effects on behavior. Neurotransmitters are the chemical messengers in our brains that facilitate communication between neurons, ultimately influencing our thoughts, emotions, and actions.

In this subchapter titled "Neurotransmitters and Their Effects on Behavior" from the book "From Instinct to Influence: Unraveling Human Behavior," we delve into the fascinating world of neurotransmitters and their role in shaping our behavior. This content aims to engage a wide-ranging audience, including individuals from all walks of life, as well as professionals and enthusiasts in the field of behavior.

To begin, we explore the fundamental neurotransmitters that greatly impact our behavior. Serotonin, for instance, is known for regulating mood, appetite, and sleep. Imbalances in serotonin levels have been linked to depression, anxiety, and even eating disorders. Dopamine, on the other hand, plays a pivotal role in our reward and pleasure systems, influencing motivation, focus, and addiction. By understanding these neurotransmitters, we gain insight into the underlying mechanisms that drive our behaviors.

Moreover, we investigate how neurotransmitters interact with one another to create a delicate balance within our brains. The interplay between excitatory and inhibitory neurotransmitters, such as glutamate and GABA, significantly impacts our cognitive functions, memory, and emotional stability. Through this exploration, we gain a deeper understanding of the intricate web of neurotransmitters that govern our behavior.

Furthermore, we discuss the impact of neurotransmitter dysregulation on various behavioral disorders. For instance, individuals with low levels of serotonin often experience symptoms of depression, while those with inadequate dopamine function may exhibit impulsive and addictive behaviors. By shedding light on these connections, we empower readers to recognize the potential underlying causes of certain behaviors and seek appropriate interventions.

To conclude, "Neurotransmitters and Their Effects on Behavior" is an essential subchapter that unravels the intricate relationship between brain chemistry and our actions. By grasping the influence of neurotransmitters on behavior, readers will gain valuable insights into their own actions and the behaviors of those around them. Whether you are an individual seeking self-improvement or a professional in the field of behavior, this subchapter will undoubtedly provide a comprehensive understanding of the role neurotransmitters play in shaping human behavior.

Hormones and Behavior: The Endocrine System's Influence

Our behavior is a complex interplay of various factors, and one significant player in this intricate game is our endocrine system. The endocrine system consists of glands that produce and release hormones into the bloodstream, which then travel throughout the body to influence various physiological processes, including behavior.

Hormones are chemical messengers that communicate information between different parts of the body. They regulate a wide range of behaviors such as aggression, reproduction, stress response, mood, and even decision-making. Understanding the influence of hormones on behavior can provide us with valuable insights into our own actions and those of others.

One prominent hormone known for its impact on behavior is testosterone. Often associated with masculinity, testosterone plays a vital role in the development of male reproductive organs and secondary sexual characteristics. It also affects aggression levels, dominance, and competitiveness. Research suggests that higher levels of testosterone may lead to more assertive behavior, while lower levels may contribute to feelings of passivity.

Another hormone that significantly influences behavior is oxytocin. Often referred to as the "love hormone," oxytocin is involved in social bonding, trust, and empathy. It is released during physical contact, such as hugging or cuddling, and can enhance feelings of closeness and attachment. Oxytocin is not limited to romantic relationships; it also plays a crucial role in maternal-infant bonding and is believed to strengthen the bond between parents and their children.

Stress, a ubiquitous aspect of modern life, can have a profound impact on behavior. The endocrine system responds to stress by releasing cortisol, commonly known as the "stress hormone." In small doses, cortisol helps us cope with challenges, but chronic stress can lead to an overproduction of cortisol, resulting in negative effects on behavior and overall well-being. Prolonged exposure to high cortisol levels may contribute to anxiety, depression, and impaired decision-making.

Understanding the intricate relationship between hormones and behavior is crucial for comprehending the complexities of human nature. While hormones play a significant role, it is essential to acknowledge that behavior is also influenced by other factors, such as genetics, environment, and personal experiences. By unraveling the intricate connections between hormones and behavior, we can gain a deeper understanding of ourselves and others, leading to more empathy, compassion, and informed decision-making.

In conclusion, the endocrine system's influence on behavior is vast and multifaceted. Hormones such as testosterone, oxytocin, and cortisol play crucial roles in shaping our actions and reactions. By understanding these influences, we can gain valuable insights into human behavior and foster a better understanding of ourselves and those around us. So, the next time you find yourself wondering why you or someone else behaves a certain way, remember that hormones may be playing a significant role.

Chapter 4: The Psychological Factors in Human Behavior

Personality Traits and Their Impact on Behavior

Understanding human behavior is a fascinating endeavor that can shed light on the intricate workings of the human mind. In our quest to unravel the complexities of behavior, it is essential to explore the role of personality traits and their profound impact on how individuals think, feel, and act. This subchapter delves into the fascinating world of personality traits and examines how they influence our behavior.

Personality traits can be defined as enduring patterns of thoughts, feelings, and behaviors that distinguish individuals from one another. These traits form the building blocks of our unique personalities and shape the way we interact with the world around us. They provide valuable insights into the consistency and predictability of our behavior across various situations.

One of the most widely accepted models of personality traits is the Big Five model, which encompasses five major dimensions. These dimensions include openness to experience, conscientiousness, extraversion, agreeableness, and neuroticism. Each dimension represents a spectrum, with individuals falling somewhere along the continuum for each trait.

Openness to experience reflects an individual's willingness to embrace new ideas, creativity, and intellectual curiosity. Conscientiousness is associated with traits such as organization, responsibility, and self-discipline. Extraversion refers to the degree of sociability, assertiveness, and outgoingness. Agreeableness encompasses traits like compassion, cooperativeness, and empathy. Lastly, neuroticism relates to emotional stability or instability.

These personality traits exert a profound influence on our behavior. For example, individuals high in conscientiousness are more likely to be organized, goal-oriented, and dependable. On the other hand, those scoring low on agreeableness may exhibit more competitive and assertive behaviors.

Understanding the impact of personality traits on behavior can have significant implications for various fields, including psychology, sociology, and human resources. By identifying an individual's personality traits, we can gain insights into their strengths, weaknesses, and potential areas for growth.

Moreover, recognizing the role of personality traits in behavior can enhance our understanding of interpersonal dynamics. By considering individual differences in traits such as extraversion and agreeableness, we can better navigate relationships, resolve conflicts, and foster effective communication.

In conclusion, personality traits play a crucial role in shaping our behavior. They provide a framework for understanding the consistency and predictability of human actions. By studying and appreciating the impact of these traits, we can gain valuable insights into human behavior, enhance our relationships, and promote personal growth.

Cognitive Processes and Decision Making

In the intriguing realm of human behavior, we find ourselves constantly making decisions. From the simplest choices, like what to wear or eat, to more complex ones that have significant consequences, such as career paths or life partners, our decision-making process plays a crucial role in shaping our lives. At the core of this process lie our cognitive processes, which allow us to analyze, evaluate, and ultimately choose the best course of action.

Cognitive processes refer to the mental activities that enable us to acquire, process, and retain information. These processes include perception, attention, memory, language, and problem-solving, among others. Understanding how these processes influence our decision-making can shed light on our behavior and help us make better choices.

Perception, for instance, determines how we interpret and make sense of the world around us. Our senses gather information, which is then filtered through our cognitive processes to create our perception of reality. This individual perception greatly affects how we make decisions, as we tend to rely on our subjective understanding of a situation.

Attention is another crucial cognitive process that affects decision-making. Our ability to focus on relevant information while ignoring distractions plays a significant role in the quality of our decisions. The more attentive we are, the more accurate and informed our choices become.

Memory is also intimately connected to decision-making. Our past experiences and knowledge stored in memory influence the way we evaluate options and predict outcomes. Our ability to recall relevant information helps us make informed decisions, while our biases and selective memory can lead to flawed judgments.

Language, as a cognitive process, enables us to communicate, analyze, and reason. Our ability to articulate our thoughts helps us weigh pros and cons, consider different perspectives, and engage in logical reasoning. Effective communication and critical thinking enhance our decision-making skills.

Problem-solving, a cognitive process rooted in our ability to think creatively and analytically, is essential for making well-informed decisions. It involves identifying obstacles, generating innovative solutions, and evaluating their feasibility. Cultivating problem-solving skills can significantly improve our decision-making abilities.

Understanding the intricacies of cognitive processes and their impact on decision-making can empower us to make more conscious choices. By recognizing the role perception, attention, memory, language, and problem-solving play, we can become more aware of our own biases, expand our thinking, and make decisions that align with our values and goals.

In conclusion, cognitive processes are the fundamental building blocks that shape our decision-making. By unraveling these processes and exploring how they influence our behavior, we can gain invaluable insights into our choices and make more informed decisions. Whether you are a behavioral enthusiast or simply intrigued by the complexities of human behavior, understanding cognitive processes and decision-making is key to unlocking the vast potential within each of us.

Emotional Intelligence and Its Role in Behavior

Emotional intelligence, a term coined by renowned psychologist Daniel Goleman, refers to the ability to recognize, understand, and manage our own emotions, as well as effectively navigate and respond to the emotions of others. In recent years, research has shown that emotional intelligence plays a significant role in shaping human behavior. Understanding this concept is crucial for anyone seeking to gain insight into their own actions and interactions with others.

Our emotions are powerful forces that influence our thoughts, decisions, and behaviors. When we possess a high level of emotional intelligence, we are better equipped to handle life's challenges, build stronger relationships, and make more informed choices. By being in tune with our emotions, we become more self-aware, allowing us to recognize our strengths, weaknesses, and triggers that may lead to certain behaviors.

Furthermore, emotional intelligence enables us to manage our emotions effectively. Rather than being controlled by our feelings, we can regulate them, channeling them in productive ways. This self-regulation is essential in preventing impulsive or destructive behaviors and instead encourages more constructive and positive responses.

But emotional intelligence is not limited to self-awareness and self-regulation; it also encompasses our ability to empathize with others. By understanding and sharing in the emotions of those around us, we can build stronger connections and relationships. This empathic understanding allows us to respond appropriately to others' emotions, supporting them during difficult times and celebrating their joys.

In the realm of behavior, emotional intelligence also plays a significant role in decision-making. When we are emotionally intelligent, we can make more rational and informed choices, considering both our emotions and those of others. This ability to make sound decisions based on a comprehensive understanding of emotional cues is particularly crucial in leadership roles or any situation where our actions impact others.

Developing emotional intelligence is a lifelong journey that involves self-reflection, empathy, and continuous learning. By cultivating these skills, we can enhance our interactions with others, foster healthier relationships, and ultimately lead more fulfilling lives.

In conclusion, emotional intelligence is a vital aspect of understanding and shaping human behavior. By recognizing and managing our own emotions, empathizing with others, and making informed decisions, we can navigate life's challenges with greater success and build stronger connections with those around us. Whether you are a student, professional, parent, or simply someone interested in personal growth, developing emotional intelligence is a valuable endeavor that will positively impact all areas of your life.

Chapter 5: Social Influences on Human Behavior

Socialization and Its Effects on Behavior

Introduction:

In this subchapter, we will delve into the fascinating topic of socialization and its profound impact on human behavior. As social beings, we are constantly influenced by our surroundings, interactions, and relationships with others. Understanding the process of socialization can provide us with valuable insights into how our behavior is shaped and how we can navigate the complex dynamics of human interaction.

The Process of Socialization:

Socialization is the lifelong process through which individuals acquire the knowledge, values, norms, and behaviors necessary to participate effectively in society. It begins at birth and continues throughout our lives, shaping our attitudes, beliefs, and actions. At its core, socialization involves learning and internalizing the social norms and expectations of our culture, family, and community.

The Influence of Socialization on Behavior:

Socialization plays a crucial role in shaping our behavior in several ways. Firstly, it helps us develop a sense of self-identity, allowing us to understand our place within society and differentiate ourselves from others. Our interactions with family, friends, and peers contribute to the formation of our personality and individuality.

Secondly, socialization influences our behavior by teaching us the appropriate ways to act in different situations. We learn social norms, etiquette, and moral values that guide our actions and help us navigate social interactions smoothly. These learned behaviors become ingrained in us, shaping our habits, decision-making processes, and overall conduct.

Furthermore, socialization impacts our behavior through the process of social control. As we internalize societal expectations, we become aware of the consequences of deviating from accepted norms. This awareness leads us to regulate our behavior accordingly, as we strive to gain acceptance and maintain harmonious relationships within our social circles.

The Effects of Socialization on Behavior:

The effects of socialization on behavior are far-reaching. It influences our communication skills, empathy, and ability to understand and interpret social cues. It also shapes our attitudes towards authority, gender roles, and cultural practices. Additionally, socialization impacts our ability to adapt and function in diverse social environments, fostering a sense of belonging and inclusion.

Conclusion:

In conclusion, socialization plays a vital role in shaping human behavior. It encompasses the process through which we acquire the necessary skills, values, and behaviors to participate effectively in society. By understanding the impact of socialization on behavior, we can gain valuable insights into ourselves and others, enabling us to navigate social interactions with empathy, respect, and understanding.

Whether you are interested in psychology, sociology, or simply improving your own interpersonal skills, exploring the effects of socialization is an essential aspect of unraveling human behavior.

Conformity and Obedience: The Power of Peer Pressure

Introduction:
In our journey to unravel human behavior, it is crucial to explore the fascinating aspects of conformity and obedience. As social beings, we are often influenced by the people around us, and this influence can shape our beliefs, actions, and decisions. Understanding the power of peer pressure allows us to gain valuable insights into the complex dynamics of human behavior.

The Nature of Conformity:
Conformity can be defined as adjusting one's behavior or beliefs to match those of a group. As humans, we have a natural inclination to fit in and be accepted by our peers. This desire for social approval can lead us to adopt certain attitudes, values, or actions, even if they contradict our personal beliefs. It is important to recognize that conformity can have both positive and negative effects on our behavior.

The Factors Influencing Conformity:
Several factors contribute to the power of peer pressure and our tendency to conform. One such factor is the need for social validation and acceptance. We often conform to avoid rejection or to be part of a group, even if it means compromising our own values. Additionally, the size and unanimity of the group also play a role in shaping our conformity levels. The more people agree on a particular belief or action, the stronger the pressure to conform.

The Role of Obedience:
Obedience, on the other hand, refers to our compliance with authority

figures or rules. From a young age, we are taught to obey our parents, teachers, and other authority figures. This learned behavior continues into adulthood, where we often follow instructions without questioning them. Obedience can be a powerful force, sometimes leading individuals to engage in actions that they would not otherwise choose.

The Milgram Experiment:
One of the most famous studies on obedience is the Milgram Experiment. In this experiment, participants were instructed to administer electric shocks to a fellow participant, even though they believed it was causing harm. The results were shocking, as a significant number of participants obeyed the authority figure's instructions, demonstrating the extent of obedience in certain situations.

Conclusion:
Understanding conformity and obedience helps us comprehend the intricate workings of human behavior. By recognizing the power of peer pressure, we can make more informed choices and encourage positive behavior within ourselves and our communities. It is crucial to strike a balance between conformity and individuality, ensuring that our decisions align with our values, rather than blindly following the crowd. As we navigate the complexities of human behavior, let us strive to be mindful of the influence of conformity and obedience, empowering ourselves to make conscious choices that reflect our true selves.

The Impact of Culture on Behavior

Culture plays a significant role in shaping human behavior. From the way we communicate to the values we hold dear, our cultural background influences our actions and decisions in profound ways. Understanding how culture impacts behavior is crucial for individuals seeking to navigate the complexities of human interactions and relationships.

One of the most prominent ways in which culture affects behavior is through language. Language not only serves as a means of communication but also reflects the values, beliefs, and norms of a particular culture. The words we choose, the idioms we employ, and even the tone we use are all influenced by our cultural upbringing. For example, in some cultures, direct and assertive communication is valued, while in others, a more indirect and harmonious approach is preferred. These cultural differences in communication style can lead to misunderstandings and conflicts if not recognized and accommodated.

Another aspect of behavior that is heavily influenced by culture is social norms. These are the unwritten rules that govern how individuals should behave in a given society. These norms dictate everything from appropriate dress codes to acceptable behavior in social settings. For instance, in some cultures, it is customary to greet others with a handshake, while in others, a bow or a kiss on the cheek is more appropriate. Failure to adhere to these social norms can result in social ostracism or disapproval.

Cultural values also shape behavior by defining what is considered important or desirable within a society. Values such as individualism, collectivism, or materialism have a profound impact on the decisions individuals make. For instance, in individualistic cultures, personal success and achievement are highly valued, whereas in collectivist cultures, the well-being and harmony of the group take precedence. These cultural value systems influence not only our career choices but also our relationships and priorities in life.

It is important to note that culture is not static but rather evolves over time. As societies become more interconnected, cultural boundaries become blurred, leading to the emergence of multicultural identities and behaviors. This interplay between different cultures further highlights the complexity of human behavior.

Understanding the impact of culture on behavior is essential for everyone, regardless of their background or profession. Recognizing and appreciating cultural differences can help foster empathy, improve communication, and promote harmonious relationships. By embracing diversity and being mindful of cultural influences, individuals can navigate the complexities of human behavior with greater understanding and respect.

Chapter 6: Developmental Psychology and Behavior

Childhood Development and Its Influence on Behavior

Introduction:
Childhood is a critical phase of development that sets the foundation for an individual's behavior throughout their life. Understanding the impact of childhood development on behavior is essential for all individuals, as it helps us comprehend our own actions and those of others. In this subchapter, we will explore the various aspects of childhood development and how they shape our behavior.

The Formation of Personality:
During childhood, our personalities begin to take shape. Our experiences, interactions, and environment play a crucial role in shaping our behavior. As children, we start to develop certain traits and tendencies, such as introversion or extroversion, that influence how we interact with the world around us. Understanding these early influences can help us better understand our own behavior patterns and those of others.

Cognitive Development:
Childhood is a time of rapid cognitive development. As we grow, our ability to think, reason, and solve problems improves. This cognitive development greatly impacts our behavior, as it influences how we perceive and interpret the world. For example, a child who has not yet developed the ability to see things from another person's perspective may struggle with empathy, leading to certain behavioral tendencies.

Socialization and Peer Influence:
Childhood is also a period of intense socialization, where children learn to navigate social interactions and form relationships with their peers. The relationships we form during our childhood greatly influence our behavior. Positive peer relationships can contribute to healthy social behavior, while negative ones may lead to issues such as aggression or social withdrawal. Understanding the impact of peer influence can help us foster positive relationships and promote healthy behavior.

The Role of Family:
Family plays a crucial role in childhood development and its influence on behavior. The dynamics within the family unit, parenting styles, and the level of support received all impact a child's behavior. For example, a child raised in a nurturing and supportive environment is more likely to develop positive behaviors, such as empathy and self-confidence.

Conclusion:
Childhood development is a complex process that significantly influences our behavior. By understanding the various factors at play during this critical phase, we can gain insight into our own behavior and those of others. Recognizing the impact of childhood development on behavior allows us to approach interactions and relationships with empathy and understanding, fostering a more harmonious and compassionate society. Whether we are parents, educators, or simply interested in human behavior, understanding childhood development is essential for personal growth and creating a positive impact on the world around us.

Adolescence and the Challenges of Behavioral Changes

Introduction:
Adolescence is a critical period in an individual's life when they undergo profound physical, emotional, and psychological changes. These transformations can often lead to challenges in behavior, causing confusion and frustration for both adolescents and those around them. Understanding the challenges faced during this stage is crucial for parents, educators, and anyone interested in human behavior. In this subchapter, we will explore the intricacies of adolescence and delve into the various behavioral changes that accompany this crucial phase of development.

Physical and Hormonal Changes:
Adolescence marks the transition from childhood to adulthood, and with it comes a surge in physical and hormonal changes. The body undergoes rapid growth, leading to increased height, weight, and changes in body shape. Hormones such as estrogen and testosterone flood the system, affecting mood, sexual development, and behavior. These biological changes contribute significantly to the challenges faced by adolescents as they navigate their new reality.

Emotional Turmoil:
Adolescence is often characterized by emotional turmoil. The combination of hormonal fluctuations, societal expectations, and the search for identity creates a perfect storm of emotions. Adolescents may experience mood swings, heightened sensitivity, and increased irritability. They may also struggle with self-esteem, body image issues, and peer pressure. These emotional challenges can manifest in

behavioral changes such as rebellion, risk-taking, and experimentation with substances.

Identity Formation:
During adolescence, individuals embark on a journey of self-discovery, seeking to establish their unique identity. This quest for self-identity often leads to experimentation, exploration, and questioning of societal norms and values. Adolescents may challenge authority figures, question rules, and engage in behaviors that may seem unconventional. These changes in behavior are integral to the process of identity formation and should be understood as a natural part of adolescent development.

Social Influences:
Adolescents are heavily influenced by their peers and social environment. They strive to fit in, seek acceptance, and establish their place within various social groups. This desire to belong can lead to behavioral changes, including conformity, risk-taking, and the adoption of new attitudes and values. Understanding the impact of social influences on behavior is crucial for fostering healthy development and guiding adolescents towards positive choices.

Conclusion:
Adolescence is a transformative phase filled with challenges and opportunities for growth. The behavioral changes experienced during this period are a result of biological, emotional, and social factors. By understanding and supporting adolescents through these changes, we can help them navigate the challenges they face and emerge as confident, responsible adults. This subchapter offers insights into the complexities of adolescent behavior, enabling parents, educators, and

individuals interested in human behavior to better guide and support adolescents during this critical stage of life.

Aging and Its Effects on Behavior

Aging is an inevitable part of life that affects every one of us. As we grow older, our bodies and minds undergo various changes that can have a significant impact on our behavior. Understanding the effects of aging on behavior is essential for individuals of all ages, as it helps us navigate the challenges and opportunities that come with getting older.

One of the most notable effects of aging on behavior is a decline in physical abilities. As we age, our bodies naturally become less agile and flexible, leading to decreased mobility and strength. This decline in physical prowess can affect behavior in numerous ways. For instance, older adults may need more time to complete tasks or require assistance with certain activities. It is crucial for individuals and society as a whole to be patient and understanding, providing the necessary support for older adults to maintain their independence and dignity.

Moreover, aging can also have an impact on cognitive abilities, including memory, attention, and problem-solving skills. It is common for older adults to experience mild cognitive decline, such as occasional forgetfulness or difficulty concentrating. However, it is crucial to note that these changes do not necessarily indicate the onset of serious cognitive impairments like dementia or Alzheimer's disease. Nevertheless, understanding and accommodating these changes in behavior can significantly improve the quality of life for older individuals.

In addition to physical and cognitive changes, aging can also influence emotional and social behavior. Many older adults experience feelings of loneliness and isolation, particularly if they live alone or have lost loved ones. It is important for society to recognize the need for social connections and support systems for older adults, as these relationships play a vital role in maintaining mental and emotional well-being.

Furthermore, aging often brings about a shift in priorities and perspectives. Older adults may find themselves reflecting on their lives, pursuing new hobbies, or seeking new sources of fulfillment. This change in behavior is a natural part of the aging process, as individuals adapt to new stages of life and redefine their sense of purpose.

Understanding the effects of aging on behavior is crucial for individuals of all ages. By recognizing and accommodating these changes, we can create a more inclusive and supportive society for older adults. Whether it is providing physical assistance, fostering social connections, or embracing new opportunities, our behavior towards aging individuals can have a profound impact on their overall well-being and quality of life.

Chapter 7: Abnormal Behavior: Causes and Treatments

Understanding Psychological Disorders

Psychological disorders are complex conditions that affect millions of individuals worldwide. They encompass a wide range of mental health issues, including anxiety disorders, mood disorders, personality disorders, and many others. This subchapter aims to provide a comprehensive understanding of various psychological disorders, shedding light on their causes, symptoms, and potential treatments. By delving into the intricacies of these disorders, we can develop a deeper appreciation for the complexities of human behavior.

To comprehend psychological disorders, it is essential to recognize that they are not simply a result of personal weakness or character flaws. These disorders are influenced by a combination of biological, psychological, and environmental factors. Genetic predispositions, brain chemistry imbalances, traumatic life experiences, and ongoing stressors can all contribute to the development of psychological disorders.

Symptoms of psychological disorders can manifest in various ways, often leading to significant impairment in daily functioning and overall well-being. Individuals with anxiety disorders may experience excessive worry, panic attacks, and avoidance of certain situations. On the other hand, mood disorders, such as depression and bipolar disorder, are characterized by persistent feelings of sadness, hopelessness, or extreme mood swings. Personality disorders, like borderline personality disorder or narcissistic personality disorder, involve rigid patterns of thinking, behavior, and interpersonal difficulties.

The impact of psychological disorders on individuals, their relationships, and society as a whole cannot be underestimated. However, it is crucial to remember that these disorders are treatable, and recovery is possible. Various therapeutic interventions, such as cognitive-behavioral therapy, medication, and support groups, can help manage symptoms and improve overall quality of life.

By understanding psychological disorders, we can foster empathy, reduce stigma, and provide support to those affected. It is important to note that everyone's experience with psychological disorders is unique, and a holistic approach is necessary for effective treatment. Cultivating a supportive and inclusive environment is crucial in addressing these conditions and promoting mental well-being.

In conclusion, psychological disorders are complex conditions that affect individuals from all walks of life. By gaining a deeper understanding of these disorders, we can foster empathy and provide support for those in need. It is our collective responsibility to promote mental health awareness and ensure that individuals with psychological disorders receive the care they deserve. Together, we can unravel the mysteries of human behavior and work towards a more inclusive and compassionate society.

The Biological and Environmental Factors in Mental Illness

Understanding the intricate workings of the human mind is a complex and fascinating endeavor. In the quest to unravel human behavior, it is crucial to examine the biological and environmental factors that contribute to mental illness. This subchapter delves into the underlying mechanisms that shape our behavior and sheds light on the interplay between our biology and environment.

Biological factors play a pivotal role in mental illness. Our genetic makeup, for instance, can predispose us to certain conditions. Research has shown that certain genes are associated with an increased risk of mental disorders such as depression, schizophrenia, and bipolar disorder. However, it is important to note that genetics alone do not determine our mental health; rather, they interact with environmental factors to shape our overall well-being.

Furthermore, brain chemistry and structure are integral components in understanding mental illness. Neurotransmitters, the chemical messengers that facilitate communication between brain cells, can become imbalanced, leading to various disorders. For instance, a deficiency in serotonin, a neurotransmitter known for regulating mood, is often associated with depression. Similarly, structural abnormalities in certain brain regions have been linked to conditions like obsessive-compulsive disorder and post-traumatic stress disorder.

While biology sets the stage, environmental factors also exert a profound influence on mental health. Early life experiences, including childhood trauma, abuse, or neglect, can have long-lasting effects on mental well-being. Adverse childhood experiences have been shown to increase the risk of developing mental disorders later in life. Additionally, social determinants such as socioeconomic status, access to healthcare, and social support systems significantly impact mental health outcomes.

Understanding the intricate interplay between biological and environmental factors is crucial for effective treatment and prevention strategies. Recognizing the genetic predispositions and neurobiological vulnerabilities can inform targeted interventions, such as medication or therapy. Moreover, addressing environmental factors like reducing stigma, providing adequate resources, and promoting healthy lifestyle choices can contribute to better mental health outcomes.

In conclusion, the biological and environmental factors in mental illness are multifaceted and intertwined. Our genetic makeup, brain chemistry, and structure provide a foundation, while environmental influences shape our mental well-being. By comprehensively examining these factors, we can gain valuable insights into human behavior. Through awareness, understanding, and effective interventions, we can pave the way for improved mental health outcomes for everyone.

Therapeutic Approaches to Treating Abnormal Behavior

In the pursuit of understanding human behavior, it is crucial to explore therapeutic approaches that can effectively address abnormal behavior. This subchapter will delve into the various methods employed by professionals to treat such behavior and provide an overview of their effectiveness.

One widely recognized therapeutic approach is psychotherapy, which involves a trained therapist helping individuals explore their thoughts, emotions, and behaviors. Through techniques such as cognitive-behavioral therapy (CBT), therapists help patients identify and challenge negative thought patterns that contribute to abnormal behavior. CBT has shown remarkable success in treating conditions like anxiety disorders, depression, and phobias.

Another approach is medication, often used in conjunction with psychotherapy. Psychiatric medications, such as antidepressants or antipsychotics, can help regulate neurotransmitter imbalances in the brain. This approach is particularly effective for individuals with conditions like schizophrenia or bipolar disorder, where a chemical imbalance plays a significant role.

For individuals who may not respond well to traditional therapy, alternative approaches like art therapy or animal-assisted therapy (AAT) can be highly beneficial. Art therapy utilizes creative processes to help individuals express their emotions and gain insight into their behavior. AAT, on the other hand, involves interacting with animals to improve social skills, reduce anxiety, and enhance overall well-being.

In recent years, holistic approaches to therapy have gained popularity. These approaches focus on treating the individual as a whole, considering the interconnections between the mind, body, and spirit. Techniques such as mindfulness meditation, yoga, and acupuncture have shown promising results in reducing stress, improving self-awareness, and promoting emotional well-being.

It is important to note that the effectiveness of therapeutic approaches may vary depending on the individual and the specific condition being treated. What works for one person may not work for another, highlighting the need for personalized treatment plans and ongoing evaluation.

In conclusion, there are several therapeutic approaches available to address abnormal behavior. From traditional psychotherapy to alternative methods like art therapy or AAT, professionals have developed a range of techniques to help individuals navigate their challenges. The key lies in finding the right approach, tailored to the individual's unique needs and circumstances. By taking a holistic and personalized approach, professionals can make significant strides in unraveling the complexities of abnormal behavior and supporting individuals on their journey towards improved mental well-being.

Chapter 8: The Role of Motivation in Human Behavior

Intrinsic and Extrinsic Motivation

Understanding the factors that drive human behavior is crucial for achieving personal growth and success in various aspects of life. Two key types of motivation play a significant role in shaping our actions and decisions - intrinsic and extrinsic motivation. In this subchapter, we will delve into the depths of these motivational forces and explore their impact on human behavior.

Intrinsic motivation refers to the inner drive that compels individuals to engage in activities purely for the pleasure and satisfaction they derive from the task itself. It is an inherent desire that arises from within, without any external rewards or incentives. Whether it's pursuing a hobby, learning a new skill, or simply engaging in a favorite pastime, intrinsic motivation fuels our passion and enthusiasm. People driven by intrinsic motivation find joy in the process and are more likely to persevere, even in the face of challenges.

On the other hand, extrinsic motivation stems from external factors such as rewards, recognition, or punishments. This type of motivation arises when individuals are driven by external pressures or the desire to attain specific outcomes. For instance, an employee working diligently to receive a promotion or a student studying hard to earn good grades are examples of extrinsic motivation. While external rewards can be effective in triggering short-term behavior change, they may not sustain long-term commitment or foster genuine passion.

Understanding the interplay between these two types of motivation is crucial in harnessing human behavior effectively. While extrinsic motivation can provide initial impetus, it is the intrinsic motivation that truly sustains lasting dedication and satisfaction. Cultivating intrinsic motivation requires tapping into personal interests, values, and passions, aligning them with our goals and aspirations. When individuals feel a sense of autonomy, competence, and relatedness in their pursuits, intrinsic motivation flourishes, leading to enhanced performance and fulfillment.

In conclusion, intrinsic and extrinsic motivation are powerful forces that shape human behavior. While extrinsic motivation may offer short-term benefits, it is the intrinsic motivation that fuels long-term commitment and satisfaction. By understanding the interplay between these two motivational forces, individuals can unlock their true potential and achieve personal growth. Cultivating intrinsic motivation and aligning it with our goals allows us to pursue activities that bring us joy and fulfillment, leading to a more purposeful and rewarding life journey.

This subchapter aims to provide valuable insights into the intricacies of intrinsic and extrinsic motivation, empowering readers to harness these forces and unravel the complexities of human behavior. Whether you are a student, professional, or simply curious about human behavior, understanding these motivational drivers is essential for personal growth and success in various spheres of life.

Maslow's Hierarchy of Needs and Behavior

Understanding human behavior has been an enduring quest for psychologists, social scientists, and curious individuals alike. In this subchapter, we delve into one of the most influential theories in the field – Maslow's Hierarchy of Needs. Developed by renowned psychologist Abraham Maslow, this theory provides valuable insights into the driving forces behind human behavior and the factors that influence our choices and actions.

At its core, Maslow's Hierarchy of Needs proposes that human behavior is primarily motivated by a hierarchical arrangement of needs. According to Maslow, individuals strive to fulfill these needs in a sequential manner, with each level building upon the previous one. The hierarchy is divided into five distinct levels, namely physiological needs, safety needs, belongingness and love needs, esteem needs, and self-actualization needs.

The first level, physiological needs, encompasses our basic biological necessities – food, water, shelter, and sleep. As these needs must be met for survival, they serve as the primary motivators of behavior. Once physiological needs are satisfied, safety needs come to the forefront. These include personal security, stability, and protection from harm. For example, people may seek a stable job, a safe neighborhood, or insurance coverage to fulfill their safety needs.

Moving up the hierarchy, the third level encompasses belongingness and love needs. Humans are social beings, and the desire for affection, friendship, and intimacy drives behavior at this stage. This need for love and acceptance often leads individuals to form relationships, join social groups, and seek emotional connections.

Next, esteem needs emerge, encompassing the desire for recognition, respect, and self-worth. People strive for achievements, success, and admiration from others, as these factors contribute to their sense of self-esteem. Finally, the pinnacle of Maslow's Hierarchy is self-actualization, where individuals strive to reach their full potential, fulfill their unique purpose, and find personal fulfillment.

Understanding Maslow's Hierarchy of Needs can provide invaluable insights into human behavior across various contexts and niches. By recognizing the fundamental drivers behind our actions, we can better comprehend why people behave the way they do and tailor our approaches accordingly. Whether you are studying psychology, working in the field of behavior analysis, or simply curious about the intricacies of human behavior, this subchapter will equip you with a comprehensive understanding of Maslow's Hierarchy and its implications.

From Instinct to Influence: Unraveling Human Behavior offers a comprehensive exploration of various theories, including Maslow's Hierarchy of Needs, to shed light on the complex dynamics that underlie our actions. By examining the interplay of instinct, environment, and social factors, this book provides a holistic perspective on human behavior. Whether you are a student, a professional, or simply intrigued by human behavior, this subchapter will undoubtedly broaden your understanding and empower you to navigate the intricate world of behavior with confidence.

Goal Setting and Achievement: The Power of Motivation

Motivation is the driving force behind our actions, pushing us to strive for greatness and achieve our goals. Whether it's climbing the corporate ladder, excelling in academics, or simply leading a healthier lifestyle, setting goals and staying motivated is crucial to our success. In this subchapter, we will explore the profound impact that goal setting and motivation can have on our behavior and overall achievements.

Setting goals provides us with a clear direction and purpose. It allows us to outline our aspirations and create a roadmap to success. Without goals, we often find ourselves wandering aimlessly, unsure of what we truly want to achieve. By defining our objectives, we give ourselves something to strive for, something to work towards. This sense of purpose fuels our motivation, propelling us forward even in the face of challenges and setbacks.

The power of motivation lies in its ability to push us beyond our limits. It taps into our innate desire for growth and improvement, encouraging us to push past our comfort zones. When we are motivated, we are more willing to take risks, invest effort, and persist in the face of adversity. It keeps us focused, determined, and committed to our goals, even when the going gets tough.

However, motivation is not a constant state. It ebbs and flows, and there are times when we find ourselves lacking the drive to pursue our goals. This is where the art of goal setting comes into play. By setting specific, measurable, achievable, relevant, and time-bound (SMART) goals, we can enhance our motivation and increase our chances of success. SMART goals provide us with a clear target, allowing us to track our progress and celebrate milestones along the way. They break down our larger objectives into smaller, manageable tasks, making the path to achievement less overwhelming.

Moreover, the power of motivation can be amplified by finding our "why." Understanding the deeper reasons behind our goals provides us with a sense of purpose and fuels our motivation. By connecting our goals to our core values and passions, we create a powerful driving force that propels us forward.

In conclusion, goal setting and motivation are essential elements in determining our behavior and achieving our desired outcomes. By setting clear goals, staying motivated, and understanding our "why," we unlock the potential within us to overcome obstacles, persist in the face of adversity, and ultimately achieve our dreams. Whether it's in our personal or professional lives, harnessing the power of motivation through goal setting can lead us on a path of growth, fulfillment, and success.

Chapter 9: The Influence of Media on Human Behavior

Media Consumption and Its Effects on Behavior

In today's interconnected world, media consumption has become an integral part of our daily lives. From television shows and movies to social media platforms and news outlets, we are constantly bombarded with information and entertainment. But have you ever stopped to think about how media consumption can influence our behavior?

The impact of media consumption on behavior is a topic that has garnered significant attention in recent years. Numerous studies have explored the relationship between media exposure and its effects on various aspects of human behavior. Whether we realize it or not, the media we consume has the power to shape our attitudes, beliefs, and actions.

One of the most significant ways in which media consumption affects behavior is through the cultivation theory. This theory suggests that prolonged exposure to certain media content can shape our perception of reality, leading us to adopt the values, beliefs, and behaviors portrayed in the media. For instance, constant exposure to violent media content has been linked to increased aggression and desensitization towards violence.

Additionally, media consumption can influence our social behavior. Through social media platforms, we have the ability to connect with others and share our thoughts, ideas, and experiences. However, studies have shown that excessive use of social media can lead to feelings of social isolation, anxiety, and even depression. The constant comparison to others' lives and the pressure to present a perfect image can take a toll on our mental well-being and behavior.

Moreover, media consumption can also impact our purchasing behavior. Advertising has long been recognized as a powerful tool in influencing consumer behavior. Companies invest millions of dollars in creating persuasive advertisements that appeal to our emotions and desires, ultimately shaping our purchasing decisions. From catchy jingles to celebrity endorsements, the media plays a significant role in shaping our consumer behavior.

It is important for everyone to be aware of the potential effects of media consumption on their behavior. By understanding the power of media influence, we can make conscious decisions about what we consume and how it may impact our attitudes, beliefs, and actions. Developing media literacy skills can help us critically analyze the messages conveyed through media and make informed choices.

In conclusion, media consumption has a profound impact on human behavior. From cultivating our perception of reality to influencing our social behavior and consumer choices, the media we consume shapes our thoughts and actions. By being mindful of the potential effects of media consumption, we can strive for a healthier, more balanced relationship with media and make informed decisions about its influence on our behavior.

Advertising and Consumer Behavior

In today's fast-paced world, advertising has become an integral part of our daily lives. Whether we realize it or not, we are constantly bombarded with advertisements that influence our behavior as consumers. Understanding the relationship between advertising and consumer behavior is crucial if we want to make informed choices and avoid being manipulated by clever marketing strategies.

One of the most significant ways that advertising impacts consumer behavior is by creating awareness and shaping perceptions. Through various mediums such as television, radio, and social media, advertisers are able to reach a wide audience and introduce new products and services. By carefully crafting their messages, advertisers can influence how consumers perceive a brand, product, or service, ultimately influencing their purchasing decisions.

Moreover, advertising also plays a key role in creating desires and aspirations among consumers. Through persuasive techniques and emotional appeals, advertisers tap into our desires for success, happiness, and social acceptance. They create a sense of need and convince us that their products or services can fulfill those needs. This can result in impulse purchases and a shift in our buying patterns.

Another important aspect of advertising and consumer behavior is the use of psychological tactics. Advertisers often employ techniques such as scarcity, social proof, and fear of missing out to create a sense of urgency and encourage immediate action. By leveraging our innate psychological tendencies, advertisers can push us towards making purchases we may not have otherwise made.

Furthermore, advertising can also influence our perception of social norms and values. Through clever storytelling and visual imagery, advertisers shape our understanding of what is considered desirable and acceptable in society. They create a sense of belonging and identity associated with their products, leading us to align our behavior with these perceived norms.

As consumers, it is essential to be aware of the impact advertising has on our behavior. By understanding the tactics used by advertisers, we can develop a critical mindset and make more conscious choices. It is important to question the claims made in advertisements, consider alternative options, and evaluate our actual needs before making a purchase.

In conclusion, advertising has a profound influence on consumer behavior. It shapes our perceptions, creates desires, and taps into our psychological tendencies. By understanding the strategies employed by advertisers, we can navigate the world of advertising more effectively and make choices that align with our true needs and values. Developing a critical mindset and being aware of the power of advertising is essential in today's consumer-driven society.

The Impact of Social Media on Behavior

In this digital age, social media has become an integral part of our lives, revolutionizing the way we communicate, connect, and share information. From Facebook to Instagram, Twitter to Snapchat, social media platforms have transformed the way we interact with one another and have undoubtedly left a profound impact on human behavior. This subchapter aims to explore the various ways in which social media has influenced our behavior, both positively and negatively.

One of the most significant impacts of social media on behavior is its ability to connect people from all walks of life. It has broken down barriers of distance and time, allowing individuals to communicate effortlessly and instantly, regardless of their geographical location. This has fostered a sense of global community, facilitating the exchange of ideas, cultures, and experiences. People are now more aware of global issues and are actively participating in discussions and movements, all thanks to the power of social media.

However, it is essential to acknowledge the negative influence social media can have on behavior as well. With the rise of social media, there has been an alarming increase in cyberbullying, online harassment, and the spread of misinformation. The anonymity provided by social media platforms empowers individuals to engage in harmful behavior without facing immediate consequences. This has had a detrimental effect on mental health, self-esteem, and overall well-being, particularly among vulnerable populations such as teenagers.

Moreover, social media has also impacted behavior in terms of self-presentation and validation. Many individuals feel compelled to present an idealized version of themselves on social media, leading to the emergence of a culture driven by comparison and seeking validation through likes, comments, and followers. This constant need for external validation can have detrimental effects on mental health, leading to feelings of inadequacy, anxiety, and depression.

In conclusion, social media has undoubtedly left a lasting impact on human behavior. While it has connected individuals and facilitated the exchange of ideas, it has also given rise to cyberbullying and unhealthy validation-seeking behaviors. It is crucial for individuals to use social media responsibly, being mindful of the impact it can have on themselves and others. By understanding the potential consequences of our actions online, we can harness the positive aspects of social media while mitigating the negative effects, ultimately shaping a healthier and more compassionate digital society.

Chapter 10: The Future of Human Behavior Studies

Advancements in Neuroscience and Behavior Research

In the rapidly evolving field of neuroscience, remarkable advancements have been made in understanding the intricate relationship between the brain and human behavior. These breakthroughs have revolutionized our understanding of how we think, feel, and act, shedding light on the complex mechanisms that drive our behaviors.

One of the most significant advancements in neuroscience is the advent of brain imaging techniques, such as functional magnetic resonance imaging (fMRI) and electroencephalography (EEG). These technologies have enabled researchers to observe the brain in action, providing unprecedented insights into the neural processes underlying behavior. By mapping brain activity, scientists have been able to identify specific regions that are activated during various tasks and emotions, helping to unravel the mystery of human behavior.

Moreover, advancements in neuroscience have also revealed the plasticity of the brain, challenging long-held beliefs about the fixed nature of behavior. It is now widely accepted that the brain has the ability to change and adapt throughout our lives, a phenomenon known as neuroplasticity. This discovery has opened up new possibilities for interventions and therapies aimed at modifying behavior and treating neurological disorders.

Furthermore, neuroscience has made significant contributions to our understanding of mental health and psychiatric disorders. By studying the brain and its intricate connections, researchers have gained valuable insights into the neural underpinnings of conditions such as depression, anxiety, and schizophrenia. These findings have paved the way for the development of innovative treatments and interventions, offering hope to millions of individuals suffering from these disorders.

Advancements in neuroscience have also shed light on the influence of genetics on behavior. Through the study of genes and their impact on the brain, researchers have identified specific genetic markers associated with certain behaviors and traits. This knowledge has profound implications for personalized medicine, allowing for tailored interventions and treatments based on an individual's genetic profile.

In conclusion, the advancements in neuroscience and behavior research have revolutionized our understanding of human behavior. From brain imaging techniques to the discovery of neuroplasticity and genetic influences, our knowledge of the brain and behavior has expanded exponentially. These findings have tremendous implications for various fields, including psychology, medicine, and education. By unraveling the complexities of human behavior, we can strive towards a better understanding of ourselves and the world around us.

Ethical Considerations in Studying Human Behavior

Ethics play a crucial role in studying human behavior, as it involves examining the intricate aspects of individuals and society. Understanding the ethical considerations in this field allows researchers, scholars, and professionals to conduct their work responsibly, while ensuring the well-being and rights of the individuals being studied. In this subchapter, we will explore the various ethical considerations that arise when studying human behavior.

One of the primary ethical considerations is informed consent. Respecting the autonomy of individuals is vital, and researchers must obtain informed consent from participants before conducting any study. This means providing clear and comprehensive information about the study's purpose, potential risks and benefits, and ensuring that participants understand their rights to withdraw at any time without consequences. Informed consent not only protects the rights of the individuals but also promotes transparency and trust between researchers and participants.

Confidentiality and privacy are also vital ethical considerations. Researchers must maintain the confidentiality of participants' information and ensure that their identity remains anonymous whenever possible. Respecting privacy is crucial as it protects individuals from potential harm and ensures that their personal information is not misused or disclosed without their consent.

Moreover, minimizing harm is another crucial ethical consideration when studying human behavior. Researchers need to anticipate and mitigate any potential physical, psychological, or emotional harm that participants may experience during the study. This involves conducting a comprehensive risk assessment and taking necessary precautions to protect the well-being of the participants. Additionally, researchers must provide appropriate support and resources to help participants cope with any adverse effects that may arise from their participation.

Furthermore, ethical considerations in studying human behavior extend to the dissemination of research findings. Researchers should strive to present their results accurately and avoid misrepresentation or sensationalism. Balancing the need for scientific advancement with the responsibility to protect the dignity and privacy of individuals is essential.

In conclusion, ethical considerations are vital when studying human behavior. By prioritizing informed consent, confidentiality, privacy, minimizing harm, and responsible dissemination of findings, researchers can ensure that their work upholds ethical standards and respects the rights and well-being of the individuals being studied. Embracing these ethical considerations not only fosters trust between researchers and participants but also contributes to the advancement of knowledge in the field of human behavior.

Applying Behavioral Insights for Personal and Societal Growth

In today's fast-paced world, understanding human behavior has become more crucial than ever. Whether you are a student, a professional, a parent, or simply someone interested in personal growth, grasping the intricacies of behavior can significantly impact your life. Moreover, applying behavioral insights not only benefits individuals but also holds the potential to drive positive change in society as a whole. This subchapter delves into the fascinating realm of behavioral insights and explores how they can be harnessed for personal and societal growth.

At its core, behavior is driven by a complex interplay of factors, including genetics, environment, and personal experiences. By examining these factors and the underlying psychological mechanisms, we can gain profound insights into why we think, feel, and act the way we do. When we understand our own behaviors, we become better equipped to make informed decisions, set realistic goals, and develop strategies for personal growth.

Furthermore, societal progress hinges on our ability to comprehend and influence collective behavior. By applying behavioral insights, policymakers, educators, and community leaders can design interventions that promote positive societal change. For example, understanding the psychology of decision-making can lead to the creation of effective public health campaigns, encouraging individuals to adopt healthier lifestyles. Similarly, insights into behavioral economics can inform policies that nudge people towards sustainable choices, benefiting the environment and future generations.

This subchapter will explore various behavioral theories and models, such as cognitive biases, social norms, and motivation, providing practical examples and applications for personal and societal growth. It will delve into the power of habit formation, outlining strategies to break detrimental habits and cultivate new, beneficial ones. Additionally, it will discuss the role of emotions in behavior and how emotional intelligence can enhance personal relationships and empathy.

Moreover, this subchapter will highlight the ethical considerations surrounding the use of behavioral insights, emphasizing the importance of informed consent and avoiding manipulation. It will also discuss the potential pitfalls of relying solely on behavioral interventions, stressing the need for a holistic approach that considers the individual's unique circumstances and values.

Whether you seek personal growth or aspire to contribute to a better society, the knowledge and application of behavioral insights can be a transformative tool. By understanding the intricate workings of human behavior, we can make informed choices, facilitate positive change, and create a more harmonious world for ourselves and future generations.

Chapter 11: Conclusion

Recap of Key Findings

In this subchapter, we will summarize the key findings discussed throughout the book "From Instinct to Influence: Unraveling Human Behavior." This book delves into the fascinating world of human behavior, exploring the intricate interplay between our instincts and the various influences that shape our actions and decisions. Whether you are a student of psychology, a curious individual, or someone interested in understanding behavior better, this recap will provide you with a comprehensive overview of the main takeaways.

One of the central themes explored in this book is the role of instincts in human behavior. We have delved into the primal instincts that have been hardwired into our DNA through evolution, such as the fight-or-flight response and the need for social connection. These instincts serve as the foundation for understanding why we behave the way we do in certain situations.

However, human behavior is not solely determined by instincts. We are also heavily influenced by external factors, and this book has examined some of the most prominent influences. From societal norms and cultural values to the impact of peers and authority figures, we have explored how these external forces shape our thoughts, beliefs, and actions.

Throughout the chapters, we have also highlighted the power of individual differences in behavior. Each person possesses a unique set of characteristics, experiences, and personal history, all of which contribute to their behavior. By recognizing and understanding these individual differences, we can gain insight into why people behave differently in similar circumstances.

Furthermore, the book has shed light on the influence of emotions on behavior. Emotions play a significant role in shaping our actions, decision-making, and overall mental well-being. By understanding the connection between emotions and behavior, we can better navigate our own emotional landscapes and develop empathy towards others.

Lastly, "From Instinct to Influence" has emphasized the potential for change and growth in human behavior. While instincts and external influences have a significant impact, we are not bound by them. Through self-awareness, mindfulness, and intentional actions, we can break free from negative patterns and cultivate positive behavior.

In conclusion, this subchapter has provided a concise recap of the key findings explored in "From Instinct to Influence: Unraveling Human Behavior." Understanding the interplay between instincts and influences, recognizing individual differences, acknowledging the role of emotions, and embracing the potential for change are essential factors in unraveling the complexities of human behavior. Whether you are a student, professional, or simply curious about the subject, this book offers valuable insights that can help you navigate behavior in your personal and professional life.

Implications for Understanding and Influencing Human Behavior

Human behavior is a complex and fascinating subject that has intrigued scientists, psychologists, and everyday individuals for centuries. Exploring the intricacies of why we behave the way we do and how we can influence and shape our behavior is crucial for personal growth, societal progress, and creating a better world. In this subchapter, we will delve into the implications of understanding and influencing human behavior, providing insights applicable to everyone, regardless of their background or interests.

Understanding human behavior is vital for personal development. By comprehending the underlying factors that drive our actions, we can gain self-awareness and take control of our lives. Whether it's overcoming harmful habits, improving relationships, or achieving professional success, having a deep understanding of human behavior empowers us to make more informed decisions and foster positive change.

Additionally, understanding human behavior is crucial for building stronger relationships and creating harmonious communities. By recognizing that each person is driven by their unique set of experiences, beliefs, and motivations, we can cultivate empathy and compassion. This understanding allows us to communicate effectively, resolve conflicts, and bridge cultural divides, fostering unity and cooperation.

Influencing human behavior is equally important, as it enables us to create positive change on a larger scale. By utilizing knowledge about human behavior, we can design effective interventions and policies that promote healthier lifestyles, sustainable practices, and social justice. For instance, understanding the psychology of addiction can aid in developing prevention programs and treatment strategies, while insights into human biases can help reduce discrimination and inequality.

Moreover, understanding and influencing human behavior has significant implications in fields such as marketing, education, and leadership. By understanding consumer behavior, businesses can tailor their products and services to meet customer needs and preferences effectively. Educators can employ evidence-based strategies that optimize learning outcomes, taking into account the cognitive and emotional factors influencing student behavior. Leaders can inspire and motivate their teams by understanding the psychological principles that drive human performance and engagement.

In conclusion, understanding and influencing human behavior are crucial for personal growth, building strong relationships, and creating positive change in society. This subchapter has provided a glimpse into the vast implications of unraveling human behavior, applicable to everyone, regardless of their field or interests. By delving deeper into this subject and applying the knowledge gained, we can unlock our full potential and contribute to a more compassionate, prosperous, and harmonious world.

www.ingramcontent.com/pod-product-compliance
Lightning Source LLC
LaVergne TN
LVHW052002060526
838201LV00059B/3797